Big Cats

by Annabelle Lynch

W

FRANKLIN WATTS

LONDON•SYDNEY

First published in Great Britain in 2015 by The Watts Publishing Group

Series editor: Julia Bird
Series consultant: Catherine Glavina
Series designer: Peter Scoulding

Picture acknowledgements: Guido Bissattini/Shutterstock: 18-19, 22tr. Volodymyr Burdiak/
Shutterstock: front cover, 12-13, 22cl. Dennis W Donohue/Shutterstock: 6. Ehtesham/
Shutterstock: 1, 5tl. enciktat/Shutterstock: 10-11, 22cr. Isselee/Dreamstime: 5bl. Eric Isselee/
Shutterstock: 5tr. Ryan Ladbrook/Shutterstock: 5br. Maggie Meyer/Shutterstock: 8-9.
Petar Paunchev/Shutterstock: 21, 22bl. Stuart G Porter/Shutterstock: 14-15, 22tl. Stayer/
Shutterstock: 4, 22br. Julian W/Shutterstock: 16-17.

HB ISBN: 978 1 4451 3830 5
PB ISBN: 978 1 4451 3832 9
Library ebook ISBN: 978 1 4451 3831 2

Dewey number: 599

Printed in China

FSC
www.fsc.org

MIX
Paper from
responsible sources
FSC® C104740

Franklin Watts
An imprint of
Hachette Children's Group
Part of The Watts Publishing Group
Carmelite House
50 Victoria Embankment
London EC4Y 0DZ

An Hachette UK Company
www.hachette.co.uk

www.franklinwatts.co.uk

Contents

Roar!

Lions, tigers, leopards, snow leopards and jaguars are big cats. They can all roar.

Snow leopard

Tiger

Leopard

Lion

Black jaguar

5

Homes

Big cats live
in grasslands,
forests or snowy
mountains.

What big
cats eat

All big cats eat meat.
They catch other
animals to eat.

Teeth

Big cats have sharp teeth to catch and eat animals.

Fur

Big cats have thick fur. The fur can have spots or stripes.

Big cat
babies

Big cats have
babies called cubs.

Playing

Big cats love to play!
They chase each other
and play at fighting.

Rest

After playing, big cats need lots of sleep.

Zzzzzz z

Pet
cats

Pet cats are from the same family as big cats. Do you have a pet cat?

Word bank

Cubs

Fur

Pet cats

Sharp teeth

Spots

Stripes

Quiz

1. Big cats can all

a) shout
b) roar
c) talk.

2. Big cats eat

a) grass
b) apples and oranges
c) meat.

3. Big cats have babies called

a) chicks
b) cubs
c) pups.

Turn over for answers!

Notes for adults

TADPOLES are structured to provide support for newly independent readers. The books may also be used by adults for sharing with young children.

Starting to read alone can be daunting. **TADPOLES** help by providing visual support and repeating words and phrases. These books will both develop confidence and encourage reading and rereading for pleasure.

If you are reading this book with a child, here are a few suggestions:

1. Make reading fun! Choose a time to read when you and the child are relaxed and have time to share the book.

2. Talk about the content of the book before you start reading. Look at the front cover and blurb. What expectations are raised about the content? Why might the child enjoy it? What connections can the child make with their own experience of the world?

3. If a word is phonically decodable, encourage the child to use a 'phonics first' approach to tackling new words by sounding the words out.

4. Invite the child to talk about the content after reading, returning to favourite pages and pictures. Extend vocabulary by examining the Word Bank and by discussing new concepts.

5. Give praise! Remember that small mistakes need not always be corrected.

Answers

Here are the answers:

1.b 2.c 3.b

Index